STILL WATER

STILL WATER
JEWELLE GOMEZ

Clayton | Bloomington

Published by BLF Press
Clayton | Bloomington

Still Water: Poems Copyright © 2022 by Jewelle Gomez. All rights reserved. No part of this publication may be reproduced, distributed, or transmitted in any form or by any means, including photocopying, recording, or other electronic or mechanical methods, without the prior written permission of the publisher, except in the case of brief quotations embodied in critical reviews and certain other noncommercial uses permitted by copyright law. For permission requests, contact the publisher.

Printed in the United States of America

First Printing, 2022

Cover Photo: Jewelle Gomez
Cover Design: Lauren Curry

Cover Photo: Jewelle Gomez
Cover Design: Lauren Curry
Photo left to right: Grace Archelina Sportsman Morandus, Jewelle Lydia Gomez, Lydia Morandus, Dolores Minor LeClaire

ISBN Print: 978-1-7359065-3-9
ISBN Ebook: 978-1-7359065-4-6
Library of Congress Control Number: 2022931939

www.blfpress.com

*Thanks to Nancy K. Bereano for launching
my literary career and being a friend;
to Stephanie Andrea Allen for her courage and vision;
to the family I honour herein.*

And for Diane Sabin always.

TABLE OF CONTENTS

I.

11 January 20, 2021
13 Eleanor Bumpers Reminds You This is Not the Titanic
15 Running Home from School
19 Another World
21 Loving
25 Marriage Vows
27 La Rondalla
31 Lyrics
33 Coal
35 Beats
37 Happy Medusa and Reclining Sappho
39 The Kiss
43 Coloured Lesbian Poem
47 We Are Everywhere
49 Our Talk
51 Aliens Invade
55 On the NYC Subway

Interlude

59	The Streetcar Named Desire
61	The Boston Streetcar 1958
65	The Milan Streetcar

II.

69	Sediments
71	Twelve Fingers Twelve Toes
73	We Talk of Mothers
75	New Orleans 2005
77	In a Mist
81	On the Face of It
83	Only 104 Words
85	Fact Checking
87	On the Plinth
89	The Buckskin Dress
91	Alcatraz Reunion
95	More Than One
97	Pardo – Searching for a Name
103	The Naming

I.

January 20, 2021

Don't you know that talking about a revolution
Sounds like a whisper.*

It's not the same as the crackle of men losing
their grip on phantoms of the past.

It's not the sound of glass shattered or
flags rippling in a high wind.

Or even bullets dropping into their chambers
Or rage fanned like a flame in a tinder-filled room.

We hope it's a new, long-awaited oath
to protect and serve up reality.

We've painted many pavements yellow and
black, talismans to ward off evil.

Yet they draw evil to them, rollers in hand
as if making something invisible is possible.

We want to put our faith in peace, a clearly
imagined calm washing over our feet.

But a tide must go out in order
to roll back in with its cool freshness.

A chance at forgiveness, the moment of forgetting
must first to be bathed in hard light of memory.

Not to seek revenge or cast guilt
like a hungry fishing line.

The fear is our demands will
fall like your noose or whip.

The true revolution will be you embracing
your shame, bubbling beneath the crust of history.

Rising in a plume of fire and tears and
rocks crystalized with anguish.

Lava must flow sudden and scalding,
burning off false histories,

making you tough enough to recognize
lies when you hear them.

And tender enough to accept the truth
of those who've been invisible to you.

Then, the revolution will be televised:**
a soft murmur in the ears of all.

*   Thank you, Tracy Chapman
** Thank you, Gil Scot-Heron

Eleanor Bumpers* Reminds You This is Not the Titanic

"I imagine one of the reasons people cling to their hates so stubbornly is because they sense, once hate is gone, they will be forced to deal with pain."

James Baldwin

…but we are going down.
Y'all been drifting through history,
dancin' on waves, clingin' to a piece of
junk left over from the ship meetin' up
with—not an iceberg—but reality.

Sure is a winter night layin' hard on you boys.
That cold froze your brain like
one of those science things
kept in a jar, waitin' to be sliced.

There ain't no ship comin' to save you
this time. No Natives gonna
teach you how to cook a turkey.
'Course there might be a group hug
at the end. But we so far from
the end we can't even see the letter
e.

Remember how you used to apologize
to your daddy for being bad? Then
he told you to go out to the alley and
bring him back a switch. That's
where we at right now.

So let go that piece of wood floating by,
whatever it used to be. Go on,
slip down in the icy water. Swim
like crazy afore it freeze your butt.
If that happen, they got to break
your legs to put you in a box.

Come on now, you can do it.
Maybe the iciness keep you woke
not put you to sleep. Everything depends
on you keep moving.
It's not going to be pretty.
There's gonna to be some crying.
And yeah, there gonna
be pain.

***

* Eleanor Bumpers, an elderly, disturbed Black woman was killed in 1984 by police with a twelve-gauge shotgun when she resisted being evicted from her flat in the Bronx.

Running Home from School*

for Molly and Daisy
for Gracie, who was recaptured
for the stolen children imprisoned at the US/Mexico border

Jigalong sounds like a playground in a children's book
and it was until the men came in cars
to protect them from themselves.
Save them from blackness they said.
For more than half a century, sweeping
young faces into cages. Mothers left
behind with only the magic of waiting.

In this story there are three small girls,
dark smudges on the landscape
streaking past squat eucalyptus,
away from thieves who have
stolen their lives.

Small, smaller, smallest in shoes too big.
Under hard sun, crossing cracked earth
like rabbits chasing rain.
Only steps ahead of trackers who
would return them to the box meant
to trim their futures down to maids, cooks
and minders of other people's children.

They are more at ease on the land
than in the dorms they've fled:
rough chemise, tin plate of food,
'protectors' faces pinched with assurance
they know what a race needs—extinction.

On the road the girls sleep in the shade
of a myrtle tree dreaming their way
through the bush, leaving no scent
or footprints to betray their guess
at which is the road toward home.
They sleep only to dream a path
out of captivity, to learn to fly.

Taut barbed wire spans the land from here to there;
longest structure on the continent. Rabbit-proof fence
to keep pests from hindering colonial progress.
The girls dream it as a finger drawn across the rocks
and scrub brush, pointing the way.

From a distance they are so like many of us:
small on an unknown landscape pushing against
the container, following a landmark
so large, so close it's never fully seen.

There's too much to take in all at once
but each upright timber is a sign.
Crossing a thousand miles, made longer
by the smallness of their feet.

Like putting an ear to the railroad track,
feeling the fence sends the sound
of a family dreaming
their return.

Following the fence back to Jigalong,
to the magic waiting
small girls steal themselves home.

***

* In response to the film "The Rabbit-Proof Fence" which told the story of mixed race, Aboriginal children stolen from their homes in Australia by the government, a practice that only ended in 1971.

Another World*

for Trung My Hoa, Vietnamese Women's Union, who survived

Five women spaced around each other in a 'tiger cage;' the name itself an anomaly. For who could put a force of nature in a box and hope it to remain natural?

Physical space is a precious thing, unique because of emptiness or how it is filled. Land of rice and lotus as far as the eye can see or ragged craters and scorched grass devolving into mud.

When looking at a circle we see both the line that is enclosure and the opening at its center—life both contained and infinite in an elemental way. Unlike a box, which implies: enough, closed within.

Space is used to redefine that which it encloses. Think of the Amistad—Africans stacked like kindling for the Middle Passage

Think of small shoes housing women's bloody feet folded.

or padded cells

or expanses of hard scrabble land—boxes marked off
for First Nations.

Each a coffin in its own way.

When they put us in that box, space left our circle. Five of us closed in on ourselves, below ground, fallen into another world.
Hiding our eyes from the metal grating above,

We couldn't see who threw lye down to burn our arms and heads; who poked with barbed sticks and ripped our flesh.

The villagers who knew me? Or a foreign ghost infecting the land? What did it matter?

My skin peeled; scars were created which must be hidden
if I survive.

At war's end I did rise from the cage and step back up
into the world,

now a tiger with new knowledge: physical space is a sacred thing.

Every molecule of air is a world; each idea circling
through is a prayer.

***

Vivian Rothstein, a feminist who works in the American peace movement reflected on her visits to North Viet Nam in 1968 and 1992: "I can remember why I was so frightened last time I was in Vietnam. It wasn't just the U.S. bombing but the sense of having fallen into another world."

Loving

> for Mildred and Richard Loving*
> for Dolores and Peachy

The parallels imbedded like deep mud ruts in a country road;
one I wish I'd traveled to meet that couple, to learn
what allowed them see each other. Indian and coloured
living with white—an uneasy mix for my own mother
further North; but not that much later
than the Lovings.

New England is not Virginia but maybe it is when
it comes to colour. Mildred testified they burned a cross
on her lawn in the 1950s while she and Richard
fought to be a married couple in their home state.

Up north in the 1960s there was no cross,
they just burned trash in front of
my mother's flat; small orange flames
reflected in living room glass—
blaze enough to scare.

Virginia called its law a protection of 'racial integrity'
as if whiteness is a land whose borders must be
guarded. Perhaps it is.

When asked if he wanted to send a message
to the Supreme Court, Richard said tell them,
"I love my wife."

Truth so plain and simple, so complex and terrifying only
those four words convey it. My mother's husband said it
many times in the privacy of their little flat and
before our family. His own turned away,
declaring him dead when he married her.

One Christmas he gave her 20 tiny bottles of perfume,
each delicately wrapped by large, cab driver hands.
Admiring the little bows and the loving which
went into each, I saw into a deep place that words
could not reach. He made a choice to lose sisters
and sons in order to love my mother,
not much darker than him, really;
but from another universe in the mind
of their small, mill town.
Now, I imagine walking down that dry Virginia road
to that rural place that held Mildred and Richard in
their embrace even when the Sheriff would not.
They'd invite me to sit in the yard
beside a well-used tire swing to drink
a glass of sweet tea.

I'd ask them how they learned the secret
so I'd know what it meant to my mother
and how her husband felt fashioning those
ribbons.

And what it might mean to me walking on a similar road
holding hands with a woman.
She and I…loving.

***

* Loving v. Virginia – The Lovings were sentenced to a year
in prison for marrying in 1958. Following their lawsuit,
the US Supreme court struck down laws banning interracial
marriage in 1967.

〜〜〜

Marriage Vows

San Francisco Public Library 2008

They had us surrounded: the people
and law not always on our side.
Eyes: mirrors of curiosity.
Books: the past.
History sliding into now.
A photo of Harvey Milk, bare-chested
stares back at us, New York Jewish grin
there among the other tribes, the Baptists and
Yemeja, the dreamers and professional queers,
cousins of all colors. The spirit of
Grace glanced at him knowingly.
She had raised me, so no surprise
at any guest who showed.
Jazz poets and belly dancers,
Book makers or bookmakers, she
knew to expect any and all.
Especially you who has stayed
these many years
The magnetic pull we felt at first

meeting has become a tensile
thread winding through our lives.
We look in wonder at the gray
in our hair and friends who endured.
Days flipped from calendars
like shedding skin
yet they are not left behind.
Each morning
we come to the beginning of a new day*
And love urges us to remain side by side.

We come to the beginning of a new day
And love urges us to remain side by side

***

* KuPaoa from Pili Oke Ao

La Rondalla

It was only a restaurant but I miss her like I'd miss a woman.
Voluptuous, gritty, innocent, contradictory and knowing.
Plastic flowers in her hair. Dressed up in gossamer,
coloured lights adorning photographs of men
with guns and small game trophies.

She moved to the rhythm of a cleaver chopping meat
on butcher block, the precision of a knife that knows its job.
The sound, a mesmerizing bebop syncopation that
swelled with Mariachi.

Taut strings of big *guittarons* complemented the clear,
clean tenors wandering ramshackle rooms.
Each player carefully pieced together
black *charro* suits, elegant with glints of silver.
The Zapata sombrero of the lead singer rose
like a moon over us—a spotlight on the romance of song.

I miss the waitresses. Reminding me of those
I knew as a kid when I waited tables in Boston—
earthy, sharp edged, loud; at the same time silenced.
Miles of walking showed in their faces; they too had

a rhythm which kept them moving around each other
in tight quarters across uneven floors,
through the steam rising from patrons,
the grill and plates piled high.

Rondalla waitresses, some in sensible shoes, some not,
never smile unnecessarily. Arched eyebrows, lips painted
bright, hair gleaming black no matter the age—
these were their protections. Generations of brown women
'dosey-doed' with each other and the young men bussing dishes;
blue collar workers migrated up from the Americas
still seeking the essence of homeland—rhythm, color, tastes.

She was not the only Mexican restaurant in La Mission;
Or even the best. Now, there is more trendy cuisine:
vegetarian tamales for *tortilleras* like me,
burritos from a truck. And all things
wheatless, sugarless, brownless.

But nothing is like her. La Rondalla, where we drank
a pitcher of margaritas from old fashioned champagne coupes,
sitting in the booth behind the guy who'd shot
one of those rabbits in the picture above the table.

The night we celebrated alongside a life-long waitress who
marked her sixty-fifth birthday, we tried new dishes.
We hummed to the music not knowing Spanish but
it threads through us weaving her story into our spirits.

For now, La Mission is still the place for burritos,
The feminist sex toy shop, secondhand stores, funky hats,
acupuncture, greasy breakfast, old movies and gritty theatre.

But I do miss her.

Turns out *rondalla* means two things in Spanish: minstrels
like the *mariachi* players—wandering, serenading with
as much care and precision as the waitress walking or
the chef chopping.

La Rondalla also means a fable. What the cooks and waitresses
created; an enchanted story-place where despite poverty or gangs
la gente from La Mission came together to do
what all families are supposed to: eat and sing.

Now I peek in the window when I go by, wondering where
they've all gone. Have they taken their magic, their music,
their fables to a new place?

Vaya con dios, my darlin'.

♒

Lyrics

> for Janis Ian
> for Ferron
> for Joan Armatrading

There is an edge
your voice
drops down
cascading sand
infinite particles
distinct and
indistinguishable
brushing around me.

Heartbreak or triumph
anxiety or vision
it floats on the air
a golden breath.

Not simply melody or motion,
words or muscle,
but you
sifting down
hourglass
until you are concrete

Only then the words
wrap around
and open
against skin:
moths fluttering dust.

I gasp and
sound seeps in,
a vein pulsing.
Improbable pairings
conclude in places I
never expected to be
or be seen.

Your song set out:
kite or net
or mythology,
a mist in the air
I breathe

Coal

for Audre Lorde

More than two decades after
your leaving I still think of you
as a diamond emerging
from the compression of carbon,
shining and sharp
both dark and light.

It's a stone that has come to mean
both delight and death
making it difficult to enjoy
the gift from the earth.

It's not possible to see the
gleam adorning soft skin
without thinking of sweat
glistening on black backs scarred
for someone else's pleasure.
Apartheid and murder cling
to the stones as
tightly as a necklace.

Yet, it is a transubstantiation,
more important than that of myth.
Earth's fiber wrapped tightly
around itself—friction and time
until it shines
like a sun.

So too are words—simply letters
and sounds draped and packaged
around each other to emerge
unexpectedly with meaning
far beyond their size
or taste in the mouth.

Your words are those diamonds
from the earth. You are the
one who toiled, sweat and shaped;
gifting them, wrapped in a prayer–
a plea that you'll be heard.
You aim each like a scented spear
meant to pry me open;
make my earth fertile enough
to grow more words
diamond bright
diamond hard,
sweat drenched light
through a desperate time.

Beats

        for the centenary of Lawrence Ferlinghetti

I'm not reminded much
of those young men who
found each other so delicious
authorities tried to bury them.

What comes to me is
the echo of a heart
the thump of a drum;
or your typewriter
pounding out words,
embroidery thread of life.

Those open spaces between;
those hesitations
we cannot live without.

A hundred years?
A hundred.

Happy Medusa and Reclining Sappho

In a side gallery, Metropolitan Museum of Art

Like waking in an Olga Broumas poem:
coloured girl surrounded by Greek marble and repressed desire;
or stumbling into two muses at a cocktail party.
I hardly expect to recognize anyone I know; every guest
so big and famous they look different up close out of context.

I glared across the gallery at Perseus, holding Medusa's
huge head aloft, as if simple dismemberment was triumph.
How manly not to notice
she'd turned him to stone.

Eyes closed, Medusa breathed me in,
my gaze cast to the shadow she made.
A subtle undulation of the snakes around her face
and the soft turn of her mouth pointed me
toward the other.

Down the length of marble floor, Sappho supine.
Hardness made soft like the Buddha
by the craft of draping stone, by the eyes:

serene, searching. Her feet, one the size of my arm
stretch from beneath her garments.

Not the diminutive or dainty thing
biographers describe; her bigness
comforts me. One's muse should be
supersize to channel our fancies
and stay in our sight.

The two here together—however captured—
unbowed, unrepentant.
Sappho reclines a short distance from
Medusa but always in relationship;
the line of communication a laser between them.

Sappho, warrior/poet firm and shapely,
one hand relaxed on her breast knowing
Medusa always watches.

The Kiss

for Angelina Weld Grimke and Akasha Hull
"...Who will ever find me/Under the days?"
A.W. Grimke

There is no darkness like your closed door
ornate panels, thick with filigree,
soundproof, denying time.
Your fair pen finds its mark in the coal black
circle of Boston society. Sheaves of paper-thin custom
threaten to bury you. Fashion, father, negritude
slip steadily from the pile of demands,
to land on your breast, to press you more firmly
into their muting folds.

Behind the door you dare to leave whispers
of your precious, stolen breath, desire
for 'her of the cruel lips,' a fragment revealed,
evidence of unruly passion and wild sadness
in the strain to press your mouth
to the hem of her skirt.

Who decides who speaks truth,
whose lips deserve to sense the yield
of another's? It is 1920,

uptown bands are playing.
Women are dancing in starched shirt fronts
and top hats, laughing out loud with painted faces.
Abolition, the obsession of your family,
has come home to Harlem.

Every shape and shade builds to cacophony
in the newness of freedom. Many are reborn
into the singing and glorious hints of redress.
You imprint a legacy: 'crying want'
in muted tones; saffron
and lilac evocations of a secret.

The soft rustle of days passing like crisp, fiery leaves
tumbling around our feet evokes that final soil
dropping darkly onto sturdy pine. Still,
you do not write of your heart pounding,
except in solitude.

The soft scratch of pen on paper is your earth
cracking open; pages filled become a lock turning;
light falls on 'dark, dark bodies.' You,
under those days: primrose and dusk,
demure, glistening with hunger.
The dewy orchid taste of your full lips,
is thick in the air. You look surprised
when mouths finally touch for all to see.

***

*Angelina Weld Grimke (1880-1958) is a lesser known bi-racial poet whose work appeared in journals published during the Harlem Renaissance and who was the niece of the Abolitionist Grimke sisters. Her many cryptic references to her love for women survive in her unpublished letters and poems which were first written about by scholar Akasha Hull.

Coloured Lesbian Poem

I need to put the word lesbian
in a poem since many are eager
that I don't. And the words
'coloured' and 'lesbian' together
confound them as if I'd paired up
a flamingo and a bear.

I'm offered umbrellas
under which I can relax,
comfortably queer
in case the word lesbian might
give me sun stroke or
embarrass other
people of colour,
especially those still perched
suspicious on stoops back in
my old 'hood.

Don't get me wrong
I like the word queer, it's
convenient: it could mean

the Castro or Christopher Street
or a restaurant in Dog Patch,
an Off Broadway bar;
a metrosexual who gets his
nails manicured, or your former
roommate who doesn't mind being
mistaken for a lesbian.

Queer cuts down on the growing list
of letters that sit like slots
in a post office waiting for
the mail to arrive and be
slipped in, cozy as a single
idea that never changes
but, of course, it always does.

Queer does help me remember
I am not alone in my slot.
We are all connected to
another letter, another world
another way of being.
But the slot is important too.
It's a nest carefully built over years
from twigs of history and
the blood from birth and wounds.
It provides a place to rest
and reminds me I'm not a tiny bird
who steps off into the air,
then crashes to the ground
beneath the heels of others
who don't see my feathers.
The stack of nests makes

a whole. The individual ideas of
who we are creates a world that
challenges and piques interest.

So, I hug the word lesbian tight to
my breasts, where my lover rests
her head at the end of the day.

I write coloured lesbian on the pillow
that I put between my knees
in bed at night to align my hips
and keep arthritis at bay.

I paint it on my high femme
dresses so men on the
street don't mistake me for
just another bird on whom
they prey.

I sing it out when asked a question
even if the inquiry has
nothing to do with sexuality
just in case there's another
coloured lesbian in the room
who thinks she's alone.

I type it into Google search every day
then pull up the Herstory archives
and legal cases, and Mabel Hampton
hoping to create a critical mass
so that lesbian porn doesn't always
pop up first.

I wear it on a button when I visit
old people in their active living
communities just to remind them
I'll be living with them soon
and some sisters are already there.

I do love having choice:
I could be woman-identified,
a woman loving woman,
same gender loving,
or queer. Any umbrella
that might keep the wrath
of men from raining down on me.

But more, I love writing the words:
A coloured lesbian
is a coloured lesbian
is a coloured lesbian
as a more mindful Gertrude
might have said.

And saying the words
tastes good in my mouth
just like that other word,
you know…pussy!

We Are Everywhere

for astronaut Sally Ride (1951-2012)

Being a first can be a drag, overwhelming
the accomplishment itself. The talk is
of firstness as if that is the secret
ingredient to your success.

First Woman? First Queer? First left-handed?
First Native? First Muslim? First Black?
First Catholic? First Buddhist?

The path you forged that led to stepping into light is
obliterated. The dust of rejection, the well-worn
ruts repeatedly broached, the slam of closed
doors and skeptical glances are ignored.

The quality of first becomes a crown whose
glitter blinds all to the toil and heartbreak,
the secrets and soul searching
before you stumbled through the door.

But it is those impediments that need
to be highlighted: The mirror

you consulted before writing your bio
or smiling into the camera. It knows
the harsh trick of light that reveals
only a chaste profile.

Now that we know something of the secret
you held I want to see you in your gear again:
youngest woman; first 'known' lesbian
in space.

I want you to be able to take all of
yourself out there into the vacuumed
silence that is the universe.
This time your space suit will be purple.
There's a portrait of your lover painted
on the helmet.

Stars may still look distant from where you
float in the cosmos; but they are blinking
and glimmering directly at you, thrilled.
They have the perfect perspective to see all
you've endured to rest in their embrace,
where I can see you by their light.

Our Talk

for Allen Barnett (1955-1991)

Cherry Grove was a place to be naked on the beach
or the deck of a summer rental. I freed myself from
the weight of disappointments, judgement, social scorn.
Lying on my blanket I dismiss the weight of mundane baggage
And listen for waves easing in and out several yards from my feet.
Their endless roll to the horizon is as sensuous as the sun
which warms my nipples, my thighs, my belly; lulling me as if
I were safe in a cradle.

Hearing my name whispered, my eyes open, I shade them
to look up at you,
one of the few men who treasures using a soft voice. You are central
casting elegant: cream coloured linen from head to toe;
a stroller down the beach from the Pines where such outfits
are *de rigueur*.

You look like success, and you are—eyes lit with the sparkling waves
as you kneel on my blanket. How long has it been
since I've been naked in front of a man so fully clothed?
You've written of the body and its dangers so we
dress ourselves in words—matching outfits.

When we were in activist meetings you were scruffier,
and earnest, signaling agreement with me when the other men
failed to hear a woman. We both apologized for being writers
rather than soldiers. But we were all warriors using what
ammunition we had at hand.

I congratulate you on your new book—
ultimately your only book; your secret held beneath the linen.
If one smile can hold both joy and tragedy it is yours that day,
knowing the only horizon you have is closer than these waves.

You are part of a generation of beloved men who will evaporate
from my life except for what is left on the page and in memory.
Your linen, my nakedness, our talk, that even now,
bridges a space between us.

Aliens Invade

for Eileen (1951-2016)

#1. 12.20.14

4,160,000 cells released into the
wildness of your spirit
grasping together
spreading apart
learning their job anew.
They come; they go;
they come again.

#2. 1.5.15

Remember we had coffee
at Café Flore one glorious,
indulgent sunny afternoon?
After retirement, I realized
I was going to miss
a network of people
who made up my world.

Not friends I hang with
over dinner on the weekends
but those I took for granted,
ones I talked to on the telephone
when we worked on a project
for the City;
or who gave each other
professional advice.
I wanted to honour the ideas and
laughs we'd had
on those calls from my desk;
things that helped me endure.

#3   1.29.2015

Couch-surfing has a new meaning
when it is the way station between
your comfort and your pain.
Bad TV is balm for the
mind when you don't want
to rest on the sound of a
doctor's voice unable to
be cheerful even with
his expensive education.
Your body comes to know
each wrinkle and roll
of the furniture.
It becomes your
companion not your prison.
And what joy a good sofa
can be.

#4   3.20.2018

You. Gone two years.
Is that possible?
Your battle with the
aliens lost. You left
behind a beloved,
a home,
friends,
a hole in the
conscience of City Hall.

I last glimpsed you
as I waited in line
to get into the gay film festival.
Our wave to each other
was a hello not a goodbye.
Unaware there'd be no chance
for more coffee dates.
It's said people
are still alive
as long as someone
remembers them.

I think of you every time
I pass the table in the Castro
where we laughed
that sunny afternoon
in Café Flore.

≈
≈

On the NYC Subway

#1
I forsake the sweet scent of gardenia
and spice of white ginger. I turn to
the hardness of citronella
to invigorate me amidst the
draining crush of humanity
and protect me from mosquitos
which I'm sure I remember
are as large as thumbs.

#2
She's maybe eight years old
Undaunted by the heat as it
puddles around her mother's
feet and is blown toward us
like a tidal pool when the train
approaches. Her two short braids
are vibrant with barrettes.
Despite the humid drape of air
she wears a sparkling bronze,
puffy jacket over her summer dress.

I can see how happy she is
by the way she
twirls and twirls.

#3
Two brown boys seem exhausted
by circumstance
from the crown of their caps
deliberately askew
to the soles of their Nikes,
designed to make them
famous by association
with a ball player
rather than bestow
the grace of the goddess.

#4
I feel great to be big in my seat.
Another large woman of colour
book ends the seat between us,
young and queenly on her phone,
in the clothes of a medical worker.
Aligned we are a Venus flytrap.
Who dares sit himself between us?

Interlude

The Streetcar Named Desire*

Today I saw Desire: darkly painted steel,
hard bells and wheels.
Here in the morning traffic
she is thick with patches;
an antique convenience
keeping to the track.
No longer swift by the muddy
Mississippi but clanging alongside
stylish boys and girls just as determined.

Little hints at her bewitching
scent lost to the change in locale.
Only a light mist on her skin reveals
the heat-driven engine that is her name.
She speeds past those full of careless
surface motion who don't sense her
dervish of want in their midst.

This time I will be a refuge,
a stranger keeping a promise,
kindness remembered,
touching my hand to your flame,
not drawing back.

***

* San Francisco is home to a fleet of antique trolley cars
from around the world, including the streetcar named Desire
from New Orleans.

The Boston Streetcar 1958

I stare at the numbers etched above
the white woman's wrist bone.
Breath jams in my throat when
my grandmother nudges me sharp
with her elbow. Already at ten
I'm embarrassed at seeming rude.

We sit in the trolley, coloured and not,
waiting for it to pull out of the car barn
and the space becomes small. I look away
—at my shoes, adverts above our heads,
at the split seat cushions—tufts of cotton
sprouting as if waiting to be picked.

I gaze at my own brown skin, soft and
unmarked. I glance next at her other sleeve:
black cloth, cuff not frayed;
a bit too short but unremarkable.

The buttons in her lap say nothing
either…a straight march of dollops
leading up to a shock of blued white
collar at her neck. Its starkness
stops me from going further.

Our orange streetcar shakes and sways
to life, downtown adventure, by way of
Tremont Street. At each stop back
and front doors creak folding open;
odd welcome in their hinges. Saturday climbs
on board: noisy boys, beribboned girls…brown,
black, white…each a universe patched around me
like those pastel states in maps of the country.

Some sit, others balance loosely above, swaying close
on leather straps, providing cover so I may
glimpse her face. The car rolling on its track
is usually soothing but the shock of her thin wrist
recalls a war movie, black and white faces marked
by shadow a child can't understand.
Until that moment, on that trolley, the numbers
on her arm had been a dramatic fiction,
crafted from nightmares.

Today the Boston car travels Market Street,
the same clanging sway, orange
lumbering beside palm trees
three thousand miles from home.

When it passes me, even now, I see her face,
younger than my grandmother.

At a stop before ours she stepped down
to the street and looked back at me
—thin brows and firm lips framed
by limp curls that did not shine.
Her eyes dark as an empty room.

The Milan Streetcar

The loose-jointed trolley from Northern Italy
rumbles not through North Beach but the Castro.
Designed by Peter Witt, with his distinctly
Protestant name, for the flats of mid-west Ohio
she loves being on the curves of the 'F line'
whose name always evokes a smile.

Arriving first in Milan in 1928 she
seduced riders with cool modern egress,
so, they remained crisp and fashionable
carrying the light scent of baking panettone.

Now, her distinctly Italian hips roll and clang
in the one neighborhood which might live up to
the idea of runway. Handsome women,
pretty boys and all in the universe between
stroll under hot sun beneath a rainbow,
shouting and singing as if free.

Maybe some remember Mussolini,
but most not. No matter.
The car achieves the patina
of the new world. We all step
off to the street in dark glasses
glancing up Market then down,
as if a designer is clucking,
nipping and tucking
before we face the audience
that adores us.

II.

Sediments

It's essential we revere that
moment when black, red, and brown
come together—soils dusting against
each other as they sift
down a mountain.

Wherever it begins, the upheaval
reveals each stratum below, richer
for the revelation. And as the colors
tumble downward, blending,
they gather strength.

Twelve Fingers Twelve Toes

for Jeshuah Fuller

Perfect the doctors said and mentioned
you might play the piano or pitch a baseball
('cause all coloured boys do).

But it is the potential for touch
that is more significant:
The tips of your fingers moving
across the skin of someone you love,
curling around the hand of your mother,
tracing words in a book.

It is a gift those toes,
that make for more dancing,
the power to walk into a new world
and march beside others who are different.

Twelve might be a miracle when
it comes to human digits or just
an anomaly that kids will envy
and tease about mercilessly

as if that will make being special
ordinary.

When you shake hands, it will be firm
and warm, the heat of difference
infusing what you touch.

When you wave it will be a sign
to come toward you.
When you reach out you will
hold the world in your hand.

It's only a mystery not a miracle,
and you will see as time passes
that sometimes more can be more
if you make it so.

We Talk of Mothers

for Elana

Sitting in a familiar place, two friends waiting for lunch,
women in our middle years. Our lifetimes reflected
by very different roads that extend behind us.
Still, as daughters, we have much in common:
betrayal, rejection, rapprochement.
Everything less dramatic when set out
on a bright, white tablecloth.

We talk of mothers, especially now mine is gone
and yours near her end. You share a recording from
a last visit; I hear your voice in hers.
Just as sometimes my mother laughs
through my mouth.

Too often they were wrapped in their own
embrace to realise the empty spaces they left us.
Then they became the children. We, now the adults,
meet them in the middle. No longer anger no longer fear
The soup arrives to remind us of forgiveness.

∽∽

New Orleans 2005

for Henrietta & Irene

I want to be your daughter,
crescent smile dazzling and
apprehensive, for
there is always danger
with the Mississippi.
Green on my toes
atop a dank, safe step,
I look down into the many
maternal faces searching
for my own.

Beneath the surface
blood was mingled so long past
there is no separating out:
whose skin, hair, eyes
are whose.

When silt is turned over
mixing bones and names,
splintered wood, tiny seeds
and faded photographs
to whom will I belong?

A fierce storm of water,
and insensate experts
was thrust between us
leaving me by the road
in tumult and desperation.
The stench is of death
and ineptitude.

Still, you are gold like gaudy fillings
flaring across an open laugh,
catching the glint of sun,
calling me back.
You are treacherous like an
angry corner of darkness and
comforting like the
end note of a song.

In a Mist

for my grandmother Lydia
for Clayton Riley

Every Sunday afternoon
my grandmother sat in the parlour
with Bix Beiderbecke—
like a young a girl, eager and
determined, entertaining her first suitor.

They were not as different as might seem:
She the daughter of an Ioway Indian,
never the fairest one in the chorus line
tapping its way along the Black theatre circuit.

Bix, his name, mysterious
like a new wheat discovered in the field,
emerged from the plains of Iowa too,
migrated to the mythical valley of jazz
to live out the songs in his head,
mastering horn and keyboard
as if they were simple farm tools.

Sundays I curled on the couch
pretending to read the comics
as she pulled his spirit from the air,
down through years until he was
almost alive again there
beside her on the piano bench.

I watched her fingers, light on the keys,
ivory gone dark with the oil of touch
from great-grandmother,
grandmother, mother, me
teasing music into surprised
tenement rooms.

She approached Bix with awe
yet was demanding like a lover.
Pulling from him the sensual core
she knew was there. Her hands
were fluid tenderness moving
around his melody, listening for
a whisper in her ear.

His song had a halting rhythm which
rocked back on itself then thrust
out to grab the next bar—
a trapeze artist high above my head.
And she was relentless in her pursuit.

She broke each section down
pounding it out as if making bread
until the melody rose inside her
coming slow and tart with
the memory of his too early death.
Then she was ready to pay attention
not to the sheet music but
to the sound of him in her head.

Sometimes it wouldn't come.
Maybe she was tired from nights
now spent cleaning office buildings or
the age in her hands.

But most days she sparked with energy
and desire. A fine sheen of perspiration
spread across her brow and Bix
was in the house. She stepped up the pace,
searching for the rhythm,
stretching to match his.

Her fingers danced across the keys
with the elegance of her old
stage days. Like a tango
she fit her body to his notes,
threw her weight onto the piano
and took off around the room
with a song so short it seemed not
to be real.

She stayed with him for decades,
companionable and challenging.
Always working out a new approach,
sensuous hands caressing the melody
making him live.

At the piano, as in life,
she had many lovers:
Debussy, Strayhorn, the Count
But she always returned to Bix–
nimble, eternal, requited.

On the Face of It

for Grace A & L Frank

It was said that we feared
the camera would steal our souls.
So it does. Souls, deep brown
of the earth, on glossy paper.

I wondered at the photograph of an Indian I found—
then realised it was my great grandmother.
Teachers said all Indians were in the history books
or buried without graves.

She was quite alive. Ioway migrant
waiting for me to come home from school.
Her image, tossed among papers on a desk,
was from a long ago trip to California.
No tribal markings on her face
but the line of her jaw unmistakable.
She is stout like the trunk of the
palm tree behind. It is thick, lively,
wild haired but said to have shallow roots.

In the picture her gaze moves out beyond me
firmly fixed in some past sky I can't grasp
no matter how closely I examine the picture.
I wonder how much of what she tells me is
conjured in order to fill an empty space
where her roots might be.

In her eyes I can almost see the reflection of
the Ioway father and Wampanoag husband.
Each died early leaving space for her life
to come into focus and be handed to me.
Deep roots. Brown of the earth. Eyes of the sky.

Only 104 Words*

...left they say. 104 words of a language from people now vanished. Rammaytush syllables wandering as orphans at the edge of a river:

ahnah meaning mother

How do humans, born onto a fertile land evaporate as if they were fog rolling over hills? Hummingbirds, trees, soil and sun plentiful, renewed each day without those who walked among them?

meme   to kill

Ohlone fishing and tracking, collecting feathers of the eagle, living under the same sky we turn to, now disembodied like echoes.

colma   moon

Only 104 words floating on brass plaques down a cement sidewalk, not on a stream that feeds the cove, not on the wind as voices blowing from father to child; not whispers from friend to friend, nor movement through the grasses where lovers are hidden:

roretaon   fire

Dubious scholars and tourists taste the letters on their tongues, searching for sounds that will raise the dead:

    harwec   *to sing*

104 words remain, carved into brass, a metal blend, the look of gold. Brass, the stuff of coins and fittings, gears and locks.

Useful things of living. Brass that shapes into musical instruments like horns or cymbals, through which all voices can be heard:

    isha   *alive*

* The plaques line San Francisco's King Street near Giants Stadium and (supposedly) represent the remaining known words of a tribe that lived for more than 1,000 years in what is now called the Mission Bay neighborhood. Some dispute has arisen about the translations.

Fact Checking

*In March of 2020, U.S. President #45 revoked the
reservation status of the Mashpee Wampanoag.*

Are we still fighting for the land
of the free, home of the braves
who tracked through marsh grasses
carrying their ancestors with them
into battle?

Did not Mashpee fires warm us
in our wetus* and tenements
lighting the way through
grandmother stories?
And still the invaders came.

We did not fault them for
their colour, their ignorance
and barbarity. Or their empty spirit,
which must have drained away
in the ocean crossing.

History is prologue we know.
Yet can it also ignite a

new fire to catch and
burn down lies?

If I recall correctly:
sovereignty is only a series of
letters tumbled together—
Until the land is in our hands
Until we remember our mother
Until pieces of paper are respected
Until the votes are counted.

Just checking…

***

*wetus are Wampanoag wigwams

On the Plinth*

They installed a temporary handrail
on the steps going up for the sake
of older ones ascending to the platform
for the opportunity to capture an image
of living Natives standing
where 'the Indian' used to lie
awkward on his back, beneath
the hooves of manifest destiny.

I wonder where they put him
once protests about celebrating
subjugation made the Pioneer
Monument embarrassing?

I surprise myself—wishing
they'd let us take him home,
both forefather and son.
Might his bronze knees unbend
so he could stand again?
His back would be firm and straight.
His hair thick with sheen; his muscles

supple enough to command the smiles
of both women and men.

He's probably somewhere resting
after trying for so long to appear
dignified and not hopeless.
And here we stand—
four elder women
from disparate tribes
but united as we lift
his spirit to the sky.

***

* San Francisco held a ceremony, photographing contemporary Native Americans on the plinth left empty when the defeated brave was removed.

The Buckskin Dress

for my great grandmother, Gracias

At eight years old I wasn't sure
what a buck might be
even as she told the story.
But I longed to see the dress,
gift from her Ioway father
she said.

A mystery, stolen before I was born,
from a trunk in the city basement
where cobwebs hung over all remnants
of the past. I carried an image
conjured up from episodes of
Gunsmoke and the Lone Ranger.

I imagined fringe swaying around her legs
as she walked past broken bottles
blossoming in the park—her eyes on
getting to market not neglect.
Not on the second hand house dress
she always wore. The riddle of buckskin
danced on her sturdy stride like silk.

The soft rustle of hide is seductive music
as she passes. Neighbors are drawn
to the sparkle of hard-worked
beading alive at her neck.

That dress is inside my head still
where I yearn to touch its butter-
soft folds, to smell the wildness
of Iowa before it fell to those
who unsettled our lives.

Although it has been said
they live no more I want to hear
the sound of her dancing
with the Native women in a
dust filled circle,
proud of the work they wear.

Alcatraz Reunion

for Dolores Has No Horses LeClaire

Mother is a tourist visiting me
as I did her when I was a child
being raised elsewhere,
worried always
she'd forget me.

Today we pretend she taught me
how to read or ride a bicycle;
that she waited by the door for me
to arrive after school or watched me
dress for my first dance.

We act as if I were not abandoned;
as if we'd shared secrets
when I was a teen. Instead, I was
anxious the world would see me
for who I was: a girl separate
from a mother.

Boarding the ferry
we are not exactly strangers;

nor are we a fragrant recollection
of worlds lived side by side,
giving shape to each other.

We are two aging women
buying memories from
the souvenir stand
damp by the gang way,
taking snapshots that will
remind us how alike we are.

It's a cold ride and perverse
to be among those eager to
peer through prison bars to
glimpse long-passed misery;
the ghosts of anger pacing and
fear caged so close to city lights.

Only when we land does the spark
of Wampanoag and Ioway fill her eye
as it did with her mother, as it does with me.

Prairie dust and Atlantic sea grasses
unite at the precipitous Pacific shoreline—
harsh and familiar;
mapping the beginning.

Others amble up the path toward
prison lore. We go deep, beneath
the thick, crumbling walls,
where rock meets rock.
Sacred space, not prison.

We cross the distance between us
in that hard, stolen place–
Ioway and Wampanoag meeting
Ohlone, Pomo, Yurok, Hupa, Shasta and
Hopi, Modoc, Sioux, Paiute, Seminole, Menominee
Inuit, Choctaw, Lenape, Ute, Ojibwe, Maidu;
a nation of nations.
The soft shuffle of their feet
on stone is a dance certain to
bind all together.

Resting on a bench, finally we hold hands
like we might have done when I was a child,
clinging tight as if the pressure
of our palms will allow us to
read each other's pasts.

***

This poem is part of the permanent installation in the
Native American exhibit on Alcatraz.

♒

More Than One

I was the quiet one
except in school, where
I made the students laugh
and the teachers cry.
Why was I so smart? they asked…
…so smart-ass they meant.
To them I squandered my talents
for waitressing or typing
by noticing history.

I was the abandoned one
too dark for my mother
too fat to work in television
too light for the Black movement
too kinky-haired for the tribe.

I was the mixed one who spoke
of only a single ingredient;
fitting myself into the times
leaving the rest for TV westerns.

I was the femme one
who could have sex with a
vice cop or a diplomat
to put myself through school.
As long I wasn't on the street
it felt much like a date.

I was the queer one
with no discernible type
except butch:
black white brown,
in no particular order.

Then I was given a name
and learned I was not a one
but many. Carrying my generations
wrapped like a precious blanket around me
woven from Ioway, Wampanoag
and Cabo Verde threads.
Wearing my wampum
not trading it. Still
making some laugh,
and some cry.

Pardo* – Searching for a Name

Gracias Archelina Sportsman Morandus.
That was a name of distinction,
many syllables full of life
and she was. Maybe named in gratitude
for her father Archibald, the horse trainer.
He forgotten, except for his dramatic death:
a kick from the hoof of one he was paid to bend
to the saddle. The horse and he now bound together
in the myth his daughter recounts to me
when I'm a girl who's been taught
all Indians are dead.

But not the Ioway, who called themselves
Bah-Ko-Je, people of the gray snow,
even as they were removed from place to place.
They are still here if only in his
grateful daughter and the earth
she has carried through the corn fields,
past the burial mounds to me.

And here in that name, Sportsman,
she said, called for his training of horses

that can kill. This makes him real;
opens the eyes of the Indians in my head.

Gracias Archelina Sportsman Morandus,
small, not healthy it seemed and
losing her father so young,
they married her off to another Indian,
half a nation away. And when he died,
leaving her the one Ioway in Massasoit territory,
she was told all the Indian nations were dead
or at the very least there had been
too many to be named.

From Gracias the memory of horses fades
like ink from paper until the time came
for her to tell the story to me.

Lydia Sportsman Morandus, her daughter.
There's a name. Her father, from Wampanoag lands,
mother and daughter, light of two nations.
And the name Lydia called after one of the nieces
who sat by the side of a sachem.

As Gracias was solemn Lydia sparkled.
As Gracias toiled, relentless and solid,
Lydia danced and sang. She was the tall, Red one
on the end of the chorus line among the Coloured.
The Black ones, paradoxically fair, testifying to the mixture
required of entertainers. Mulatto, mestizo, pardo,
No darker need apply.

In the distance between Ioway and footlights,
even with the years that grew between her
and the corn fields, between her and the horses
Lydia, her skin earthly copper heated from within,
kept her name always.
She repeated the stories to me
in her mellifluous song.

Dolores Morandus Minor LeClaire.
There's a name that begins with sorrow.
Dolores, child of Lydia, my mother.
Although she discovered early: the burden
of a darker daughter was too much for her.

As Gracias and Lydia were fire, warm as a hearth
and the stories told around them, Dolores was
forever a girl not to be encumbered.
She was an infectious laugh ringing in a room
with too little furniture, no blankets or chairs.
No place for a small child to hold on.

But in the end, she was the one
to pick up the trail of her fathers.
Through New England sand dunes and
grasses she sifted and surfed, clicking
on the strands of information while she
still had sight. Then touching and talking
to those with the stories.

She yearned for that history
to fill the empty room inside of her.

She pulled, hand over hand, scaling the side
of a mountain on a fragile thread
until she found a name that was hers.

There in cool, eastern shadows,
in the dust of history, among the faded
writing on government paperwork,
she found the Indians who are not dead.

They saw her and the corn fields left behind,
her and her mysterious grandfather
with his ropes and hooves. They saw her
and the women who came before.
Taking away her sorrow, they named her:
Has No Horses,

Has No Horses,
not because she was poor and blind
but in honor of her laugh.
Has No Horses because
she had no need to go to people,
they would come to her.

Say her name out loud and
hear her laughter almost as warm
as a story; big and round,
full of pasts overlapping and
contradicting each other.
It's a name I'll remember
now that the women,

my small nation,
are all gone.

And my name is still to come.

***

* Pardo was a 12th century Portuguese word often used for darker races, sometimes it meant earth-coloured, sometimes it meant an in-between color, sometimes it meant gray.

♒

The Naming

for my sister/friend Mineweh

1.
Deep, you said.
Not like we did in the sixties looking
for meaning in random signs
or gems or yogis. Deep,
as in waves cutting a channel
through rock, shaping new land.

We met at the bed of my mother, dying
with a grandeur lacking in life.
Mother, who'd always loved strays
more than she loved me, searched
for our history and found a guide
to her grandmothers. And to her name
which had been stolen
when Pilgrims came ashore
'discovering' and divining.
They determined to turn us to
a suicide they called religion
burning our language along
with our wetus.

They harpooned whales
with ease and forgetfulness,
overplanted the soil and
swallowed lives
like starving children.

Their great task—making the Bible
into Wampanoag to complete our death.
Scriptures heavy upon our heads meant
to bury our spirits and our bodies.

Although, today it yields one silver thing:
a dictionary to revive our words
and return them to
the lips of children.

2.
The East is cold; once an idea is frozen
it remains forever the same
or it cracks and is lost
as it seemed were the Wampanoag.
But we were not.
Now we turn toward home with the
ease of a horse staying on its path,
the language of its road well-trod.

We gathered in a New England yard
many colors and ages to find my name;
imagining the land 400 years ago
before synthetic fabrics
and false fires were used
to tell us our names.

At our center was a tree which hadn't
borne leaves in many years
yet it stood firm, branches spread
like a fertile net. It's spindling arms
glistened with possibility.

There you decided–
deep cut channels home to
abalone, sand dollars and starfish.

Still Water—for moving slow through stone,
leaving my trace embedded in rock, in sand,
on the pages of lives.
Still Water who touches all shores
past and present, in my journey to the ocean
even as I seem unmoving.

Lifting my name from the air that
whistled through the bare branches
you lay it across my shoulders
where it now sits
as if it were always
my own.

Ka Ana Tuk Amuk
Still Water.

About the Poet

Jewelle Gomez (Cabo Verdean/Wampanoag/Ioway) is a playwright, novelist, poet and cultural worker who was born and raised in Boston, MA. She lived in New York City for 22 years before moving to the Bay Area. She received her BA from Northeastern University in Boston and an MS from Columbia Graduate School of Journalism. She was on the original staff of one of the first weekly Black television shows, *Say Brother*, at WGBH TV in Boston (1968-71).

She's the author of eight books including three poetry collections and the first Black Lesbian vampire novel, *The Gilda Stories*. It was the winner of two Lambda Literary Awards and has been in print continuously for more than 30 years. It was recently optioned by Cheryl Dunye (*Watermelon Woman*, *Lovecraft Country*) for a television mini-series.

Her most recent plays were commissioned by New Conservatory Theatre Center: *Waiting for Giovanni*, about an imagined moment of indecision for James Baldwin and *Leaving the Blues*, about internationally known singer/songwriter Alberta Hunter. Both premiered in San Francisco and were later produced in New York City by TOSOS.

Gomez was on the original boards of the Gay and Lesbian Alliance Against Defamation (GLAAD) and the Astraea National Lesbian Foundation. She also worked as a grant maker for 30 years.

She was the recipient of a Legacy Award from Horror Writers of America (2021); a Trailblazer Award from the Golden Crown Literary Society (2016); the Barbary Coast Vanguard Award from LitQuake (2016); and was a Lifetime Achievement Grand Marshall for the San Francisco 2019 PRIDE Parade.

Follow her on Twitter and Instagram: @VampyreVamp

To learn more about BLF Press, follow this QR Code:

www.ingramcontent.com/pod-product-compliance
Lightning Source LLC
Chambersburg PA
CBHW011318080526
44589CB00020B/2748